The ABCs of Cryptocurrency

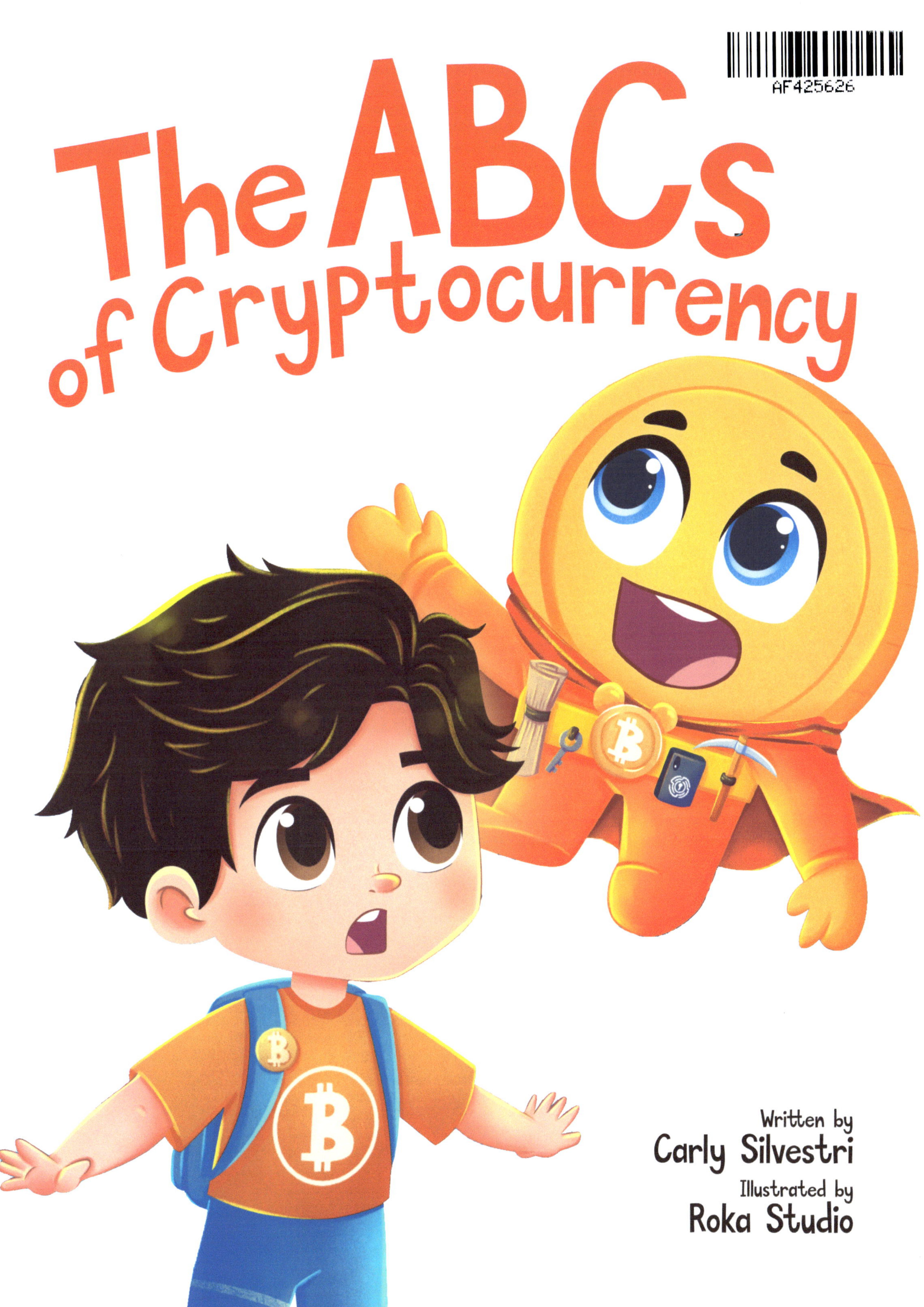

Copyright © 2026 Crypto Wonder Press LLC

Published by Crypto Wonder Press LLC
San Jose, California

cryptowonderpress.com

Hardcover ISBN: 979-8-9988328-2-6
Paperback ISBN: 979-8-9988328-3-3

Library of Congress Control Number: 2026909638
First Edition, 2026

For educational licensing and bulk orders:
hello@cryptowonderpress.com

For Brooklyn, my greatest treasure — may you always know your worth.
I wrote every word of this book for you.

And for Adam, you are in every page of this story,
in more ways than one.

Come along — it's time to see A brand-new world from A to Z.
With Bitcoin Man to guide the way, Adam is here to learn and play.

Through nodes, keys and blocks locked tight, We'll learn what makes the future bright. Open this book — your journey starts here, A crypto adventure that's fun and clear.

A is for Address
Your crypto home's a string of code,
Where coins arrive and safely load.
Check twice before they hit the road!
bc1qs3s dp49haef
bc1qs3sdp49haefx8dm9e7jkqp370qr6r045h3rngu
bc1qs3sdp49haefx8dm9e7jkqp370qr6r045h3rngu
045h3rngu
bc1q
Definition:
A crypto address is like your home address — but online!
It's a special code that tells your Bitcoin exactly where to go.

Bitcoin Man says: "Always double-check your address!"

B is for Blockchain
A growing chain, built just right.
Each block links — locked in tight.
It keeps the truth in plain sight.

Definition:
A blockchain is like a digital notebook. It records every transaction in order and once it's written, it cannot be changed.

Bitcoin Man says: "Block by block, the record grows."

C is for Coin
No clink or clank, but full of might,
It travels fast, like beams of light.
One coin holds value, secured just right.

Definition:
A crypto coin is digital money. You can send it, save it, or spend it online. Bitcoin was the first and is the most famous.

Bitcoin Man says: "One Bitcoin always equals one Bitcoin."

D is for Decentralized
No king, no throne, no single guide,
Block by block, stacked tall and wide.
Miners help the truth abide.

Definition:
Decentralized means no one person or company is in charge.
Instead, computers all over the world work together to keep
things fair and strong.

Bitcoin Man says: "No kings, no thrones—Bitcoin power to each
their own!"

E is for Exchange
One coin, two coin, three coin — four! Buy and trade on the exchange floor. Tap to trade, then swap some more!
Definition:
An exchange is a digital marketplace where people buy, sell, or trade crypto coins.
Bitcoin Man says: "Only trade with exchanges you trust!"

F is for Fork
A fork appears where paths divide,
You build, you mine, you choose your
side. New ideas begin their ride.

Definition:
A fork happens when people change how a blockchain works.
The code splits, and new ideas take their own path forward.

Bitcoin Man says: "Some forks bring change. Some bring coins.
All start something new!"

G is for Gas Fee
Send your coin — slow or fast, Pay a fee — it's crypto gas!
It powers the network, so you can pass.

Definition:
A gas fee is a small cost you pay to send crypto or use the blockchain — like a toll on a digital highway.

Bitcoin Man says: "Check your gas — it empties fast!"

H is for Hash
A hash is code that can't be cracked,
It locks each block and guards the stack.
Change one thing and it won't come back!

Definition:
A hash is like a digital fingerprint. It gives each block
a special mark.

Bitcoin Man says: "Hashes secure the block — and know when
something's off."

I is for Internet Money
Coins online, no paper to hold, Send and spend —
fast and bold! Digital treasure, stronger than gold.

Sending...

Definition:
Internet money is digital money you can send, save, and
spend online. You can use it anywhere in the world!

Bitcoin Man says: "Coins that can go anywhere!"

J is for JPEG
Pictures glowing pixel-bright,
Digital art that brings delight!
Own it with crypto — that's your right!

Definition:
A JPEG is a digital image. Some are just pictures and some are recorded on the blockchain as NFTs, making them one-of-a-kind digital art you can own and trade.

Bitcoin Man says: "A JPEG can be art — own it on the blockchain!"

K is for Key

Your crypto key unlocks the door, It gives control of all
you store. Keep it safe — it can unlock so much more.

Definition:
A crypto key is a secret code that lets you move your Bitcoin on
the blockchain. Keep it safe — because it controls your coins.

Bitcoin Man says: "Your key reveals everything — protect it well."

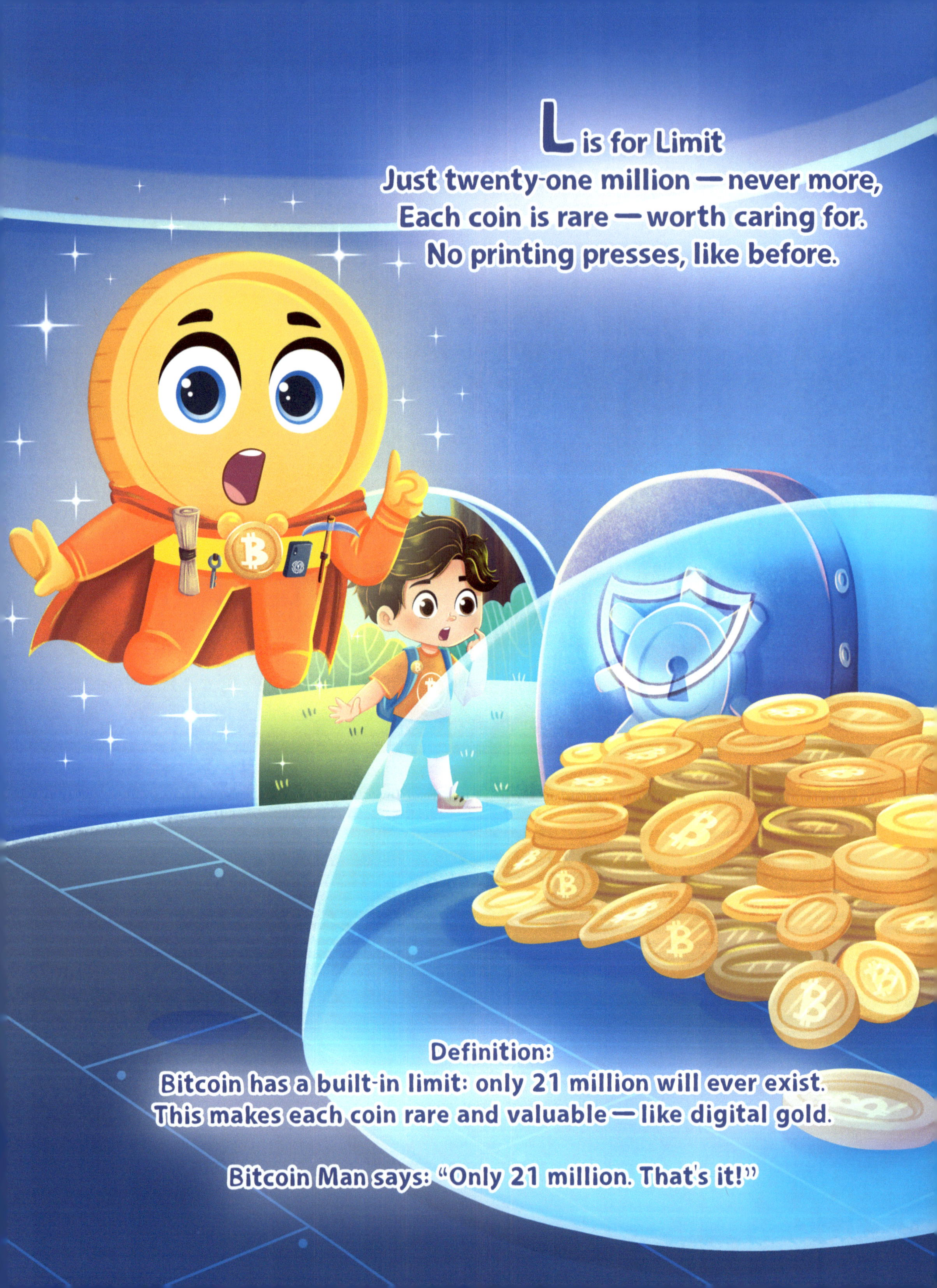

L is for Limit
Just twenty-one million — never more,
Each coin is rare — worth caring for.
No printing presses, like before.

Definition:
Bitcoin has a built-in limit: only 21 million will ever exist.
This makes each coin rare and valuable — like digital gold.

Bitcoin Man says: "Only 21 million. That's it!"

M is for Mining
Miners race to win the block,
Minting coins around the clock.
Solve the puzzle — earn the stock!

Definition:
Mining is how Bitcoin is created. Miners solve puzzles to add
blocks and earn rewards like new coins and fees.

Bitcoin Man says: "Rewards for math — that's mining!"

N is for Node
A node checks each transaction right,
It guards the chain by day and night.
It validates everything in sight!

Definition:
A node is a computer that checks and confirms transactions on the Bitcoin network. It helps keep the blockchain honest and running the right way.

Bitcoin Man says: "Nodes validate everything."

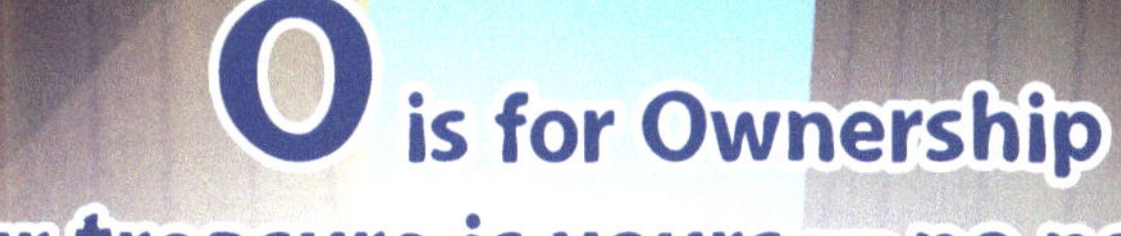

O is for Ownership

Your treasure is yours — no need to share, In Bitcoin, no bank can take what's there. Your keys, your coins, yours to keep with care.

Definition:
Ownership in Bitcoin means no bank, no company, and no government controls your money. If you hold your own keys, your coins belong to you and no one else.

Bitcoin Man says: "Guard your keys. Own your coins."

P is for Private Key
Your private key moves it all, Guarding it close is protocol.
Lose it once—you lose it all.

Definition:
A private key is a secret code that lets you send your crypto. If you
lose it or share it, your coins are gone—no one can get them back.

Bitcoin Man says: "Your private key is just for you."

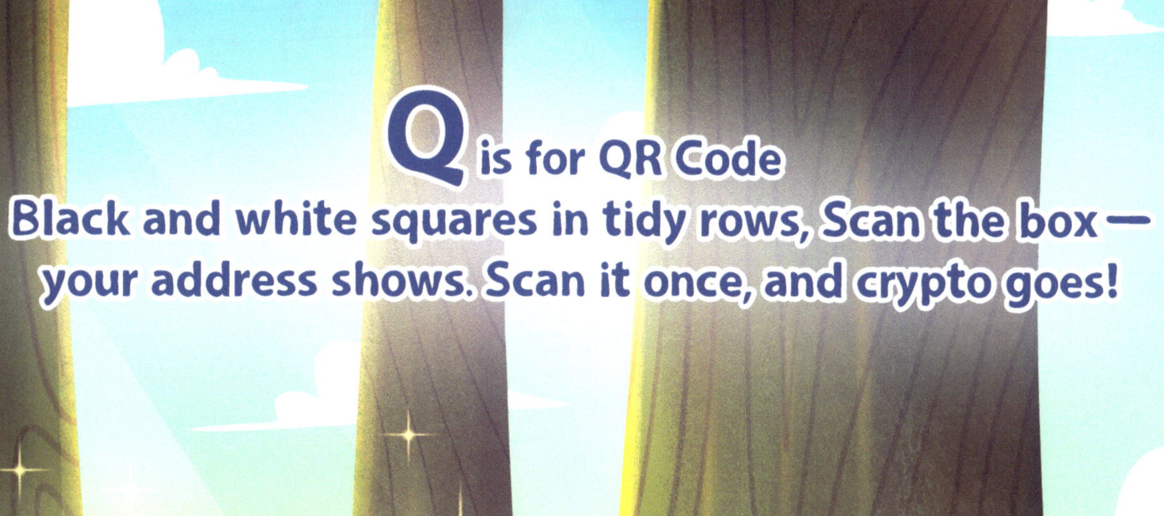

Definition:
A QR code is a black-and-white square that holds digital data —
like a crypto address. Scan it with your phone, and it fills in the
address so you can send or receive coins without typing.

Bitcoin Man says: "Scan the code — let your crypto go!"

R is for Rug Pull
Some coins seem too good to be true,
Then vanish fast without a clue.
Always check before someone scams you.

Definition:
A rug pull is when someone
creates a fake crypto project,
takes people's money, and
disappears. Always do your
research before you invest
or send crypto.

Bitcoin Man says: "If it sounds
too good to be true — it is."

S is for Satoshi
A secret name who played the biggest part, Satoshi built a world with code to impart, A quiet spark became the start.
BITCOIN
A Peer-to-Peer Electronic Cash System
Satoshi Nakamoto
satoshi@gmx.com
www.bitcoin.org
Definition:
Satoshi Nakamoto is the mysterious creator of Bitcoin. Satoshi changed money forever.
Bitcoin Man says: "Satoshi made our future grow!"

T is for Terabyte
It stores the blockchain far and wide,
A digital world is packed inside,
Where bits and bytes and blocks reside.

Definition:
A terabyte is a large unit of digital storage.
It can hold thousands of files, videos, and
even blocks from blockchains.

Bitcoin Man says: "Big blocks need big bytes."

U is for Unlock
A key unlocks what's locked away,
It starts your path, it lets you pay.
With one key — you're on your way!

Definition:
Unlock means using your private key to open
something special — like sending a coin,
accessing a wallet, or starting a digital journey.

Bitcoin Man says: "Your private key unlocks your coins."

V is for Value
Bitcoin is valued by young and old, Some spend it fast while others HODL. Digital treasure, worth more than gold.

Definition:
Bitcoin has value because people can use it like money, and only 21 million will ever exist. In crypto, "HODL" means holding your Bitcoin no matter what.

Bitcoin Man says: "Bitcoin's value is here to stay."

W is for Wallet
No Wi-Fi. No tricks. Just keys stored cold.
Write down your phrase, it's yours to hold.
Millions in Bitcoin—lighter than gold.

bc1qs3sdp49haef
x8dm9e7jkqp370q
f6m045h3rngu
35.364912358

Definition:
A wallet stores your private keys.
It lets you send, receive, and control crypto safely.
Cold wallets stay offline to keep your keys secure.

Bitcoin Man says: "Own your crypto. Own your freedom."

X is for xPub
Your wallet's xPub helps you receive,
New addresses that you can retrieve.
One shared code — hard to deceive.

Definition:
An xPub helps make new addresses to receive Bitcoin. It keeps your wallet more private and organized.

Bitcoin Man says: "One xPub — many addresses to receive!"

Y is for Yield
Your coins can grow while staying still, Some watch them with care and skill. Time and patience may pay the bill.

Definition:
Yield means earning more crypto over time.
Some people earn it by lending, staking, or saving.

Bitcoin Man says: "Hold it safe and watch it grow!"

Z is for Zero-Knowledge Proof
You show you know, but nothing's shared.
The secret stays, but you're prepared.
The math says yes — so truth is declared.

Definition:
A zero-knowledge proof lets you prove something is true without revealing the secret behind it. It's smart math that protects privacy and it's being explored in Bitcoin too.

Bitcoin Man says: "Truth can be proven — without sharing the facts."

ABOUT THE AUTHOR

Carly Silvestri is the founder of Crypto Wonder Press, an independent children's publishing company based in San Jose, California. She writes Bitcoin and cryptocurrency books for kids and families who believe the future belongs to those who understand it early. The ABCs of Cryptocurrency is one of its debut titles.

Discover more books from Crypto Wonder Press at **cryptowonderpress.com**
Follow the adventure: **@cryptowonderpress**